Between Two Windows

OLI HAZZARD was born in Bristol in 1986, and studied English at University College London and the University of Bristol. He is currently researching John Ashbery's poetry at the University of Oxford. Oli Hazzard's poetry has appeared in magazines and anthologies including *The Forward Book of Poetry 2010*, *Best British Poetry 2011*, *The Salt Book of Younger Poets* and *New Poetries V* (Carcanet).

Also available from Carcanet Press

New Poetries V: An anthology, edited by Michael Schmidt with Eleanor Crawforth

OLI HAZZARD

Between Two Windows

CARCANET

First published in Great Britain in 2012 by

Carcanet Press Limited
Alliance House
Cross Street
Manchester M2 7AQ

www.carcanet.co.uk

ISBN 978 1 84777 139 1

The publisher acknowledges financial assistance from Arts Council England

Typeset by XL Publishing Services. Tiverton
Printed and bound in England by SRP Ltd, Exeter

for Lucy

Acknowledgements

Acknowledgements are due to the editors of the following publications in which versions of some of these poems have previously appeared: *Best British Poetry 2011* (Salt, 2011), *Clinic II*, *Five Dials*, *The Forward Book of Poetry 2010*, *Horizon Review*, *Lung Jazz: Young British Poets for Oxfam* (Cinnamon Press, 2012), *New Poetries V* (Carcanet, 2011), *PN Review*, *Poetry Salzburg Review*, *The Salt Book of Younger Poets* (Salt, 2011), *The Shuffle Anthology II*, *Warwick Review*. I would also like to acknowledge the support of the Arts Council UK for a Writer's Grant I received from them in 2011.

I would like to thank Maria Hazzard, Robin Hazzard, Greg Normand, Mark Ford, Roddy Lumsden and Michael Schmidt for their encouragement, support and advice.

Contents

I

II

I

And many standing round a waterfall
See one bow each, yet not the same to all
But each a hand's breadth from the next.
The sun on falling waters writes the text
Which yet is in the eye or in the thought.
It was a hard thing to undo this knot.

Gerard Manley Hopkins

Moving In

You take me down to the crease in the hills
Where the farm's boundaries are smothered
By brambles and the dry stream-bed lies
Like a pelt – we follow it quietly, shoeless,
Listening to the waves at Calpe knead into
The beach, and reaching out my hand to
Touch your hair we are suddenly
Aware of the sensation that we are being
Overheard: yet all there is on this side
Of the valley is the fuzz of telephone
Wires overhead and darkness slowly
Encroaching behind the skin-pink clouds –
The orange trees, after all, seem to clutch themselves
Above the safflowers and alfalfas that
Spring from the ground like cocked eyebrows –
So, stepping onwards – stalking, by now –
Convinced that night is simply the folding over
Of fingers, leaned into a steeple – we hunt
For some burrow, some hood of earth
Where the sound of the sea is as unbroken
As it is within a coiled shell and build
A fire whose voice, like chicks-being-
Incessantly-hatched, will make our
Own seem all the more improbable. But
Now, as I sit alone, crumbling dry leaves
In my palm, it seems all I can dream of is
The onset of sleep. Really, I hardly notice
The rising heat of the circling brush fire that
Flays the whole sky of its stars.

The Inability to Recall the Precise Word for Something

All things are words of some strange tongue
Jorge Luis Borges

The first person you see after leaving your house
One who always wants to know what's going on
To make money by any means possible
A surgical sponge accidentally left inside a patient's body
Given to incessant or idiotic laughter
An incestuous desire for one's sister
The act of mentally undressing someone
One who speaks or offers opinions on matters beyond their knowledge
A secret meeting of people who are hatching a plot
The act of beating or whipping schoolchildren
The categorisation of something that is useless or trivial
Belching with the taste of undigested meat
One who is addicted to abusive speech
The use of foul or abusive language to relieve stress or ease pain
The condition of one who is only amorous when the lights are out
To blind by putting a hot copper basin near someone's eyes
The act of opening a bottle with a sabre
The habit of dropping in at mealtimes
The act of killing every twentieth person
One who eats frogs
The low rumbling of distant thunder
Someone who hates practising the piano
The practice of writing on one side of the paper
A horse's attempt to remove its rider
The collective hisses of a disapproving audience
The sensation that someone is mentally undressing you
The act of self-castration
Being likely to make a mistake
One who fakes a smile, as on television
Counting using one's fingers
The act or attitude of lying down
The smell of rain on dry ground
The space between two windows

True Romance

1

The window I saw myself in was a room.
The sun unpacked the buildings. On the deep table
An antique map, bleached of its colours, lay twitching in
The breeze, a drowsy mantis. I drifted beneath a honeycomb of balloons;
Mistook swans for dollops of cream; saw ghosts in
The white of Chinese-burned skin. Those people
Inside looked out at me strangely. They couldn't
Believe it when I reached out to touch them. I said, We all believe
In the value of pretending one thing is another, don't we?
We were all a little frightened. But I could not do what
I threatened. Something else was needed to secure it in place.
Said another way, maybe it could have happened.

2

Said another way, maybe it could have happened,
I threatened. Something else was needed to secure it in place.
We were all a little frightened. But I could not – what?
In the value of pretending one thing is another. Don't we
Believe it? When I reached out to touch them, I said: we all believe.
Inside looked out at me strangely. They couldn't.
The white of Chinese-burned skin, those people –
Mistook swans for dollops of cream, saw ghosts in
The breeze. A drowsy mantis, I drifted. Beneath a honeycomb of balloons,
An antique map, bleached of its colours, lay twitching.
The sun unpacked the buildings on the deep table.
The window I saw myself in was a room.

Rule of Thumb

Like any klutz cuffed in the *esposas* of a single mother tongue,
I put on gloves to throw snowballs
                    and draw blank at *vorgestern*;

and like the regular *geisterfahrer* I know to anticipate a bite
when at the tail end of a *culebra*
                    a cobra pulls into sight;

and though it's well within my *ken* to see beyond my sect,
it was only *iets door de vingers kijken*
                    I found out the way to pronounce the fact

that, though I only look in windows, I can barely look myself in the eye
knowing I might, at any moment, *fais du lèche-vitrines*
                    is, apparently, *mamihlapinatapai*.

Mid-Air

Today I place a camera high on winter's nerve.
From where I perch my hooded head
makes the sounds of birdsong
issue from the same stuffed mouth
as a car spinning wheels on ice.

I open my mouth to catch such eerie doilies
as the sky sheds. This is a place of
clouded quiet, staffed by a loose sync
of birds pursuing their own breath, bellows
pumped by invisible hands, crossing

the guttural road that curves up the hill
until it snuffs at the lip – to meet
that part of air prepared to receive
the image of your car, the image of you
in the image of the car, squinting

out through the windshield for the road's
slick shields of black ice. There's most danger
where the road shows through most clear –
where your mind will be hesitant to feel
for texture through the distant numbness

of unfamiliar wheels, nor able to trust
in the faults of their tread. Rocking backward and forward
my body presses through the polystyrene air
to remind itself of the relation of hand to glove
to glove to hand, of hand to glove to hood

to head, of the saving barriers – the icebergs
of sleepless nights, casts for swollen, broken limbs –
that keep a thing from the feel of itself. Now, I remind my
eye to keep quiet for my blood
as a fly creeps across the viewfinder.

Apologia

His stillness knows exactly what it wants. Flemish, it climbs
down the rungs of its laughter, 'til strasse-light chokes
in the key of its throat, or a reticulated fog catches
in the youngish trees; or, through the milk-bottle glaucoma
of a villainous monocle, it scouts out the gallery of a plot-hatchery
with a test-tube full of bewitching molecules. *Thwarted!* In the long hiss of its head,
thawing silence slakes the fossilising song *Their Life is Hidden with God.*

Some song! Like a soft cymbal it shirrs in the recollection.
The city's plushness crab-hands along the neck
of its buildings. Who trusts such plushness, huh? (Does *who* fuck?)
It neither declares intentions nor inters declensions.
Playing it backwards reveals a song being force-fed itself (the *tack-tock-tuck-tick*
of drool from its mouth). Scuppered, he lounges against the scene-stripping
window: tries to name, then count, then watch, the flux of birds palpitating

in the sprained lens of a lake, a jigsaw shaken out of its box,
indicating, in a shaky hand, that the shape's clear, the picture less so.
Cheap tricks earn cheap treats, brother, he mutters, before, like the sudden urge to
feign sleep, an obscure and untrustworthy impulse selects
the sensation, then turns it over to itself: do what you have to (Baltimore,
                                                                    simpatico)
but make it quick. But his stillness could outrun itself. Decades without water!
Then: We don't seem to have moved. Then: Every move an altar.

Entre Chien et Loup

I cannot separate lucidity from undressing.
                                        Lyn Hejinian

1

After years of exposure to the violence
that erupts out of competition between sounds
and lights in pursuit of my living, I have built

up enough resistance to peripheral enticements
to rail my desire secure and leisurely
as the orbit of domed plates of luminous sashimi.

Though ostensibly civilised by my refusal
to lust after what I am unable either to attract or afford,
I worry I only think I know nothing

opens at the mere mention of sesame: see how I mow on,
fish-eyed, pink-lobed, unlooping through winter's
hive-light a word that withers in the throat,

weighed down to the point of kneeling by the debt
of apparent learning. If only it were really possible
to moult a thought whole, L., I might begin everything

again: spend what little of myself I portion to fear
not fearing the consequences of not giving what is not needed,
but fearing the consequences of not giving what is.

2

The marginal delay between the sounds coming in
through the door open onto the balcony
and their emergence in the background of the news

report combine into an unbroken, wavering
chain of metal or turquoise bunting, spelling out in flickering
characters *you must wear your rue with a difference*: 'Well,

I'll do what the weathers suggest, pal, there is no
other window…' All night it rained mercury
in the tramlines, and once trustworthy-seeming

expense rocked up cow-eyed and lacking endurance.
Like any good neighbour, I took to the vista:
with a dragonish gasp I pressed my body against

the window, and felt my flesh spreading and whitening
into the Rorschach of some hideous insignia.
My skin duned at the sudden chill, and I peeled

myself away, leaving an imprint of mist and grease
that clouded and smeared the blue lungs of the plane trees.
That was when you placed your hands over my eyes.

They that conduct tailbacks in my Russian dreams, that thatch gums with lovelorn cattle-prods, that assume an anchor in a bed of sun, that stop short of hay, that plummet like tulips into the unbroken river, that are stepping too quickly into the middle of a queue, that is not moving fast enough for the yellow and green cars, that are either too miserable to face-paint today, that have to drink the colour bottle-green, that cannot play this afternoon because she stepped on a razor, that looks at the mirror as a photograph, that collate all species of pet reluctance, that teach advanced ice-cream van at the graduate school this semester are all sporting aviator jackets the colour of water.

They that let the dogs run out in the road, that have unstitched the ice cubes, that my knowing thickened into a grainy paste, that became an embassy to this bravado of blessings, that the weather cannot absorb, that decided that it, that distil deer from insurance company calendars, that reap archaisms from passport holders who, that with others did commit, that I may honour regularly clink sun-rays in bordered midnight.

They that leave love-bites upon my neck, that abhor the gathering of flies in clusters, that when the ground gave way did not, that at the culling of vertigo can laughter, that is what is meant by, that with birds & physicians ripen dunes in air before noon sink postcards into the thought of snowstorms.

They that harvest such branches from gathered lungs, that do not suffer from rheumatism or consequences, that add three salts to the night and mix, that have faces like both sides of a spoon, that design a house that spells out my name & walk around in the blueprints with their shoes on, that clean up the after, that is not quite finished with you yet young, that are atrophied insistence, that caulk the plump nest of the brain's intention, that are a quiet advocate of crunk, that pixellate their own sound as it comes when the lights go off and on very quickly cannot remember the name they should not have said.

They that cannot bear to hear you swallow, that name their larger moles & hurricanes, that begin the confidence & then have to swiftly back-track, that need affection just like anybody else, that start again this time as cautionary tale, that are both cautionary tale & advertisement for, that sits in the pocket like a foetus dreaming of rape, that are many colours at once, that none are superior to any other, that sits down in the room like hunger and has to be managed tediously, that touch me deeply with proof at the best of times remind me of being born with only four eyes.

They that are both mo her & so , that moth r & on everyone refers to by their house number, that know everything about each other's bodies, that in the purring larynx are culturally better prepared for, that ritual of chip & ketchup, that read poems deciphered from the graphite shading of the clouds, that must see the mot & s situation in this resort &, that philander disappointment, that could not miss the opportunity to feel spite in this most auspicious, that cannot sleep without the sound of traffic poured into the ear like sand, that is the worst part of everything we've seen themselves, that has been scrubbed so hard you can see through it to the grain of the sky at dawn, that is poured into the sun like hot, that security guard from has called me again, that cannot be left somewhere near the middle 8 decided to actually get up on the cymbals & start shouting.

They that lose & find their pin number in the same breath, that scorch osso bucco with flames from their fingertips, that cut their tongues on cans of grass, that is totally un, that um, that is dog-eared midday in Burgess Park could once birth a fully grown dragon in under an hour.

They that swell into a hovering blimp of summer, that cross-breed with other people's faces, that are better prepared for bad news by a film, that though they normally hate Tom Hanks, that go to all the speciality stores and talk with the assistants, that flee the knowledge that all cities are like, that stand in Trafalgar Square with a sack of fresh zebra meat, that are like a walking pregnancy test, that no one dare take, that are hus and a d w e, that a e h sband and if, that re hu b n an w fe, that squabble over the bill, that are both bill and embarrassed waiter, that are letting the rest of the salmon stay, that have arranged for a set of keys to be cut, that climb sideways through the woods, that, that have, that have slowed the cabling of fish to the surface, that sign themselves as T. Hanks and look weary, that are struggling to find funding for their cock-extension, that have a ratio of frowns to dishes ratified by the gloss of, that flense the sun's motes, that is a state-of-the-art staircase, that clambers up laughter at the last moment suck stars into a rollercoaster's ambitious first draft.

They that do not move out of lust for the reach, that are warped in the settling plain of friends, that become pursued by the liquid insistence of New York, that have to get off the bus half an hour early, that are what is obscured by the question of before he died found a way of assembling the most hurtful beauties.

They that catch the frightening of horses in their lipstuck mouths, that is essentially the ranking supervisor in this situation, that are designing a kind of you that cannot be forgotten or neglected, that live inside a set of shelled celebrations whose outer layer is barely, that is a light that does not sleep but eludes your watching between segments are suddenly able to discover their tethered polar bear, corking in the armchair.

They that are holding blue baskets swarming with diagrams & decongestants, that leave miniature vapour trails in the basin, that could deploy Horace or could not deploy Horace, that hold oysters on the tongue in lemon juice for breakfast, that run arms aloft through a downpour of pneumatic drills, that could care less about the cunt in the pram, that in what sense do you mean like a, that she could have gone anywhere with today chose for her to stay at home, that drain urgency from the sound of, that is the dried organ laid out on, that when you get close-up aren't quite as handsome as you first thought, that is nobody's fault, that tunes his skin to a roguish flush, that is exactly what I'm talking about, that are famous in this part of town but no one gives a flying fuck about in, that is another example have in accordance with demand developed ways of making one person last for over 10,000 hours.

They that before you arrive have decided how the evening would ideally progress, that scour the detritus of their remembering wholly rendered in, that is peaceful & taut & gorgeous, that are still the best way of storing thought, that is a bed sheet spilling from a window in the wind, that are better than you could ever have imagined, that are blue and brown washing tugging at a line, that are puddles disobeying gravity, that have taken your apology to, that are no less than what is pretended to, that love as the shape of summer emerges at midnight mass take down the cartoon dandelions from the tabernacle.

They that are loud talking outside the window, that are torsion in the cable, that are the radio on very quiet, that take me out for a walk around the yard, that burst into seed, that are being buried in sand the shape of a body that could not exist, that lie down between two generous slabs of olive ciabatta, that in doing not doing that, that is what, that is on the board of sever, that puff out the yews with blisters in sync, that what is the problem exactly, that bathe in birthday parties for cancer, that bombard welcome to Adriatic, that better leave the dog until it falls asleep, that scotch is free, that are unfuckable, that are unshakably second wave third shore, that stone you were thinking of picking up, that are the inflatable skyscraper, that does not bounce, that is a big mistake, that cannot use the stairwell, that as long as you're back by nine there won't be, that papier mâché landscape arranged with painted against metallic, that cannot be bought at any old shop, that is the heart of the community, that old sales technique for those, that don't take off the chain, that is losing its identity, that burst forth from the death slide with concussive pleas, that is not what I am here, that could not have been there as they were, that cannot be bled in time for the start resuscitate this fact in this crazy heat.

A Few Precepts

Always keep the end in mind.
Don't blow your brains too soon.
Premature enunciation leads to stress
for the foetus in the womb.
Mend their ways. Part what you see.
Remember: what some people call a marriage bed
some people call a tomb.
Potato potato. Pronounce scone as scone.
Pronounce grass as grass. Bastard is
as bastard does. Keep your mind
on a short leash. Don't let it eat from
the table. If it barks at you,
bark back. Lock it in a room.
If it needs to relieve itself, never put paper down.
Soon enough it'll be line-broken.
Pick up after it. Be prepared to eat shit
sandwiches. That picnic
will be no picnic. Sew someone else's name
in your pants. Make sure your friends are freedom-
range. Beware your uniform:
do not let it beware you. Drop twenty
and give yourself twenty.
Forget how many necks these woods have grown.
Only loot what you can't afford. Don't touch
yourself. Don't let your moods
get in a room together. Chew the fat
ones, then spit them out.
Drink sake for the sake
of a joke. Give your children only middle names.
If you remember nothing, you've had a good time.
If you pick at that thread
you'll be caught with your pants down.
By the time you're done, home will be the place where,
when you have to go there,
they have to report you to the relevant authorities.

Some Shadows

Sitting in the square, we hear the swing of the light
And the sudden shadows of the trees
Lash the whitewashed buildings: we are mute,
And the trees seem just expressions of their shadows
Levered up on the sun's slings. I pretend to read
And you muse inscrutably, with a curling finger

Through your beard, whose strands like coral fingers
Glow slowly in the morning light.
'Is it possible,' I ask, 'that you might read
Some warning in the difference between trees
Stood so far apart that seem as shadows
To grow together, so their shape is muted?'

In what sense might a tree speak, let alone be mute?
You reply, as you sceptically finger
The bill. 'Some things cast a tapestry of shadows
That, when seared by the strength of light,
Make palimpsests of themselves; as trees
Can't be seen without, in a sense, being read.'

How grandly you speak this morning! What did you read
That made you think you should stop being mute?
I am stung: I didn't think, in the shade of the trees,
That speech, like some drowsy, buttoning finger,
Had to be always working. I step into the light,
Leaving my share. I browse the stalls, whose shadows

Flatten in wedges the flaking shadows
Of birds flying overhead: where did I read
Of them as 'bits of burnt paper'? In some sombre light,
Through the crack of a door, when the night was mute,
And the page is 'hoarse to the lift of a finger'?
Suddenly, as though trawled through the trees

24

Of the whole continent – through the ancient trees
Of Patagonia, that fling long shadows
Like the hand of God, with his single gloved finger –
An accordion tune, its melody sight read,
Fills the square that was, only now, mute.
Its melody twists like shoals of light,

Squirming through the trees, impossibly light;
And I turn to see that you, with a stuttering finger, still read
The bill, through twitching lips that shadow words.

Pantoum in Which Wallace Stevens Gives Me Vertigo

In Wallace Stevens' poem 'The Public Square',
a languid janitor bears his lantern through colonnades
and the architecture swoons. I cannot read this poem
without being struck down with vertigo. I can only read:

'A languid janitor bears his lantern through colonnades...'
before I start to feel sick, and suddenly aware of the earth's roundness.
Without being struck down with vertigo, I can only read
whilst strapped into my chair; I will read the poem, and

before I start to feel sick and suddenly aware of the earth's roundness,
I can remind myself that it's only a poem, I'm not going to fall over
whilst strapped into my chair. I will read the poem, and
triumph by making it to the end. But this is not my ultimate goal.

I can remind myself that it's only a poem. I'm not going to fall over
myself just because of one little achievement. I don't really
triumph by making it to the end. 'But this is not my ultimate goal,'
I say – as if that were anything like the truth. Every day I celebrate

myself because of one little achievement (I don't really!)
and the architecture swoons. I cannot read this poem,
I say, as if it were anything like the truth. Every day I celebrate
Wallace Stevens' poem 'The Public Square'.

Two Versions of 'Fabliau of Florida'

1

Hop for probe-quash.
Capable hymen, tho.

Mouth a tonne. Ad overview:
Tethers a tonsil-baa,
Handles tubing.

One ear – calm a fond duo.
Trusty, solemn morons.
Gild aversions.

'Hullo,' (bray). Lick full.
I whet with no hog milt.

Hell? A bed. Intervene, wren!
Huffing thins, rooted, rots.

2

Sh. Baroque Prof., hop-
Hop. Batman. Lychee.

Oh, a retentive ovum! O, wand!
Theorise as blatant
As blighted nun,

Re: aeon. Faun-clad doom!
Stony melon rostrums,
Gravid lesions

(Back-hour filly lull).
We hit with thin gloom.

Whenever binned, retell a
Fistfight, routed on horns.

Badlands

There are no trees in the yellow foaming
Wheatfields; or maybe a single, gnarled
Birch that, Lear-like, webs the air
                with its waving limbs.

The pylons stand bow-legged, mercenary.
The wires slither towards the horizon
Bearing whispered prayers. The sky is bright
                and taut, bruised with space.

A man, as naked as if dressed in his own pelt,
Cartwheels in the nest of a cloud-shadow.
I call out to him, but his stride is unbroken.
                I read my letters.

The sun disperses its light like a lozenge: –
Its sediment quivers at my feet. I cannot
Withhold my crazy laughter as my voice
                sieves into the wind.

Four Landscapes

1

Outside in the fields it is raining
with the sound of plastic bags uncrumpling
in a palm cupped around an ear
pointed towards this coffee-coloured sea
across which a number of small boats sail
as if the dangers were no longer rational
but formed only an embarrassing example
of what hesitancies should never cross
the vellum on a distant apostle's desk.

2

Absorbed by the city's motheaten cube
I am learning about the history of Libya
the inbox choking itself with charity junk
thick miles of sunlight unrolled
an abandoned blueprint curling up on its tube
I am terrific and unable to concentrate
on the calibre of hesitation that characterises
what I imagine to be the space across which I
distinguish between thinking and speaking.

3

This being some kind of slow journey
or scenic route taking in all the sights of the local
countryside the spasm of the coastal
road displaying moments between the shrill
trees full of insects the calculable distance
of the land point shanking the sea and birds
hanging as though caught on some tether
we can relax into deep distances between speaking
floating words cut adrift from words.

4

Clouds pull apart with a doughy lightness
as we stumble out into open fields
where birds form then dissolve in the tentings
of spreathed sunlight and garbled
scrawls are lifted from the saffron-spatter
scratching out some other walker's tread
cuffs of frost wilt the edges of splayed leaves
oscitant voices dye the silence rust
the sound of blood mizzling in the lull.

Glasnost

Can you believe we were ever strangers?
I'm leaving you everything
except my corneas. This blonde turns on
the local air. The future tunes out. Look,
her computer one morning at work. Try not to breathe
don't stare. An error occurred
from the stone. I'll kill anything once.
This directive. I drink my blood straight

and living creatures. I'll stone anything –
nude clairvoyant, funeral sales.
'Are you guys having a fire down there?'
slippery slope. Frantically, she calls tech support and asks,
You may have everything except my blood.
I haven't had sex in ten years
of whatever it is you think
I've been saying. Until a familiar room

with a book of carpet samples
to distinguish texture from the appearance of it
though you never know do you with the light
frottage against diplomas. How did you overcome
your youth is a weapon, and I would just like to know
which complimentary onlookers will be cheering.
You may have the technology, but
I love you, Michael.

kendo sunray
dummy jaffa
soso parlour
roti condo

dodo dolor
foray rabies
jammy mirror
offa faker

miso solice
tiller latent
canti timber
asda dandy

doe-eyed ray-bans
mittened farming
solvent larynx
titters danger

vido cutie
dollar lotso'
puffer clammy
sundry lido

doda tipex
label sono
fatwa miaow
reagan donor

doting fido
raving hooray
melon roomie
farsi camphor

solo lasso
lava bella
tidal yeti
dovetail kiddo

brando mis'ry
yummy fluffer
corso velour
anti hairdo

donald rations
mimic fashion
solid larval
timid david

A Week in the Life

Now the morning is landlocked in its magnifying glass.
Now the afternoon is simmered to Braille.
Now the evening flakes off its plaster; pieces flap, flail.

Now the morning is floating in albumen.
Now the afternoon is wearing armbands.
Now the evening has a dead goldfish bobbing in it.

Now the morning muzzles the evening.
Now the afternoon flaps like a Post-it note with *morning!* written on it.
Now the evening rolls back in its own head.

Now morning and evening occur like phrases made from fruit machine pictures
                                        of bananas and cherries.
Now the afternoon chisels itself into its original shape.
Now the evening is bottled in the ballgown of a streetlamp.

Now the morning is what the solidness of the afternoon leans against.
Now the afternoon is half-seriously threatening someone with legal action.
Now the evening peels itself off the afternoon.

Now the morning is stretching between the poles.
Now the afternoon contains an old man screaming.
Now the evening cools to a wax lake.

Now the morning is a reflection of all other colours laid on top of one another.
Now the afternoon is the texture of a steel drum.
Now the evening springs up at you like a wave.

Are We Not Drawn Onward, We Few, Drawn Onward to New Era?

Marge, let's send a sadness telegram.
I roamed under it as a tired, nude Maori.
No trace, not one carton.

Kay, a red nude, peeped under a yak.
Was it a car or a cat I saw?
Amen, icy cinema.

Nurse, I spy Gypsies. *Run.*
No, I tan at a nation.
Flee to me, remote elf.

Eva, can I stab bats in a cave?
Oozy rat in a sanitary zoo
Loops at a spool.

Outside

All through the afternoon the sound like water pouring into bowls
fills the empty corridors of the house
like an ache spinning through a tooth
eaten, as language is eaten,
from the inside out.

An idea is meant to begin inside you.
Out in the courtyard, sun sprays through the pomegranate tree.
Shadows open like gills on the flagstone,
stir the clover of everything
too slowly in the ear.

Making it equal is too slowly like
an accident or argument. Too quickly the sound of water
falls into itself. Through the empty corridors of the house
I move like a tooth in a bowl, spat
from the inside out.

Language eats its own ideas.
In the evening sun fills the pomegranate tree.
Out in the courtyard, I'm inside or outside.
They are not equal, accident or argument. I hear water pouring
inside out.

Prelude to Growth

Tomorrow is watching today through the one-way mirror.
Something is taken from each, exchanged for something else, more
or less valuable.

Your too-thick glasses, the ones that
are totally off-trend, render the suddenly swarming pavilions
a tearful furnace.

No one is more or less orange. Microbes of sand grow
on my eyes. The collision between cement-mixer and ice-cream van
provokes less identity

in the etiolated gallantry of longhand. Make milk my measure
of white. Or today a smaller fraction of my life.
To oil that lends water a gradient.

And yet the gorgeous weather continues to move along
the walls,
plucks the Dijon telephone, approves its endurance.

Now your hand hovers
over each object: it self-inflates to meet the bruit gift.
As these beaches

remain leaning into their own portrait,
in that fuller night, our skin powdery, we see the whole event
unfolding very slowly,

the wind somersaulting down our throats.

II

But as the days and years sped by it became apparent that the naming of all the new things we now possessed had become our chief occupation

John Ashbery

Sonnet

The vast pumpkin-coach sprays ochre dust
on the finely etched grain: how many brassy-gleaming
coins flung to clatter amongst the crowds' gurgling
clishmaclaver, how many phosphorescent
torques hung…? No will's as strong
as a cloud in which a voice mumbles, engulfing
its audience with an adolescent strum, or
better yet (hoarsely now) the pyx-bound diarchy
propped upon a burnished palm! Yet over the bristling
ice-chafed land the foghorns disperse, eventually running out
of twine; the cliffs lean and shift like pale passengers
squashed against the pane; the sea shirrs
against itself, hissing, unfurled, of its irreversible wane: –
standing here, I count myself, count myself again.

As Necessity Requires

An emptiness returns to surround the books, lamps, apple-cores
and photographs, until the room is a cupboard full of cans
with their labels removed. The distended, much-thumbed reflection
is plain and repetitious, as the texture of the silence between the effort
and the inability becomes a noise rubbed so hard, and so long,
it seems to hallucinate a source upon its surface. In this slow frieze
of inertia, such mistakes are lent a barely credible uniformity,
yet fall back through the embellished openings of embarrassment
to place each one at its starting point, a fresh fixity in its gaze,
as though the distance had rolled itself up into a welcome mat
that could be covered in a single stride. So this is your home:
tell me how much you recognise. In the phlox of the brain, home means a diorama
in which the setting and the species are the same. But earliest details
are porous as the most tender plot, the peripheries bordered with
breathed-upon glass, an opportune spray of tendrils, the humid fuzz
tuned in by the elastic mollusc of an eyeball. Something in
the corner sets a clear blister in the blurring air; softens, then hardens, into
the stillness required, an outstretched hand trying to steady itself.

The required stillness descended, having run naked into the Plexiglass.
The reverberations thrummed along the windows of the other exhibits;
those with tongues to the glass picked up the low note
of slapstick misery, turned either in pity or terror to capture
the event's rotations, then reported in a manner that identified, then secured,
the syntax of their feeling; alcoves and swiftly branching passages tuned
the pulse of the air-conditioning to an arhythmical drone. And yet recesses
continue to appear in the shucked resemblances of earlier hours, their
own kind of numb learning, continuously filled with fragrant
and explosive fluids, as sunlight is pulled down into a building. These
become thoughts that don't know they're thoughts. Later, bridges
that hunt their own breaking. When it comes, it is like seeing
a memory for the first time. The easy guilt of noticing that
nothing else rises to the brim of this jar – this puffs it out a little further,
elevates it in degrees of thousands of feet, until its size is such
that to look down from it would be to fall, which would be a sort of answer,
perhaps, but to a completely different, less necessary question; of the tension
in hollowed air. Or, how large we need ourselves to become.

40

Arrival

The vibrating harp of rain drove them
sprinting into the pine wood. Made content amongst shadow
and cicada trills, they soon grew fond of the names
they'd given to the trees and animals; in night's recesses
they learned to conjure mephitic
fumes from the bomb-puckered earth,
to sing certain obscene songs;
they ran through the wood
trailing honeyed light behind themselves,
their songs wholly eaten up by silence.

Yet the stubbly meadowland drew them out one evening;
they crept on their bellies to avoid being spied,
dug their fingers into the pliant earth at the sound of
fires. The empty trees, having clutched laminate sky all winter,
suddenly sprung meat and wet clothes on their branches
(pale stars blinked awake in the gaps between) –
and until the dawn leaned over the mountains
(their rigid eyes twitched from their stare)
the extended branches of the air
carried murmuring voices far into the night.

A Walking Bird

When we wade out together
through the scrolls of brackish water, dispersing
the long rainbow-nets, the frail networks
     of foam and grease, the brief, glyptic
        reflections of branches and twigs
     spidering the surface –
'we'll need something more than this…'

So we return to the hearth
joking that death is a matter of proof, if
I'm willing to follow my argument
     through: the wind gargles itself in
        the chimney, the thunder outside
     rolls its stone across the cave-
mouth, and they retain a youth

of sorts, though only to younger
ears than yours: 'Who endures such oneiric
phenomena when there's a world outside
     to be civilised?' you say, scrunch-
        ing up papers for kindling –
     as daffodils spring from
logs, shadows roam the ceiling.

To Comprehend a Nectar

The wind flagellates
Leaves into flakes of burning
Green: like a show tune jauntily
Stippled out on a distant piano,
To-and-fro above the sun's
Shifting archipelago
They transfer their hued gaze
Upon the startled grass,
Transfixed by its tattered screed.

★

In the hour before
Dawn, a hoarse fox limps through
The moon's downy light;
Wobbling on a pergola, a seagull
Unhinges its rusted throat. Aghast, barely awake,
I fill orange bin-bags with clinquant leaves
Lifted from the lawn's loose
Snakeskin. Later,
Chain-smoking in the flowerbed, I'll watch them
Peel off like wigs from the open tops;
Watch them, wind-blown, settle back
Upon the ashen grass, gingerly composing
Inscrutable constellations.

Carapace

Confusion swells in the eroded areas:
pomade caught in the theremin
of a copse drags us out further, where a springbok
spurts over the moss and fallen leaves. All squat, cross-
legged in the brass spume; each frail leaf gets given
a name fit for the duration of its being spoken
then is filed for later address. In the long afternoons
we imagine ourselves floating over the spayed turf, a glaucous
brume thinning to mizzle on our lenses,
our vision blurred with unquantifiable speed
or slowness. In the evening, the sun slips stockings
onto the bases of trees, and all
voices meld into one loudspeaker's
drone; neither castigation nor intrigue, its tone divides
the populace into spoken for and speaking. Soon the air
fills with honeydew; some complain
of a burning sensation in the throat – others,
hailing the descent of manna, raise
a wooden glass to an incumbent. There
are no minutes to indicate the length and obscenity
of the words that follow, withdrawn into whispers until
they stall sleepily, unhooked from syntax
in the mandarin pools of a suburban
midnight, illuminating a town
divided along the flight paths of migrating birds,
where nothing is ever said twice.

The Asymmetric

The trees at night, each a black cloud
tethered to the earth, whistle and
simmer, inward, aloud – 'seeming
at once both a single soul and
a crowd': – though the asymmetric
ear persuades a drunken mind

that it is, in fact, a condensed, static
ball pawed at by the turbulent wind,
and – yes, you really did catch up nicely.
But here, as he stops to vomit, the
street lamps, sensing their opportunity,
crank up their exhausted shimmy, and the

shadows peel themselves from the tree trunks
like peering priests; and this strange process
begins, from nowhere, through which all things in
sight become plated with fiercely fixed
orange, whose thick syrup-grip seems to slow-
ly loosen the focus of his vision

like it's twisting a stiff jar lid: –
his eyes, now, are cold and blurred, as
though weighed with scales or pennies…
as the trees and streetlamps assert
themselves again, unstoppably
this time, their voices struggling

to balance – isn't there some phrase
that moves in this, like wingbeats through
leaves? Nope: amongst the Mexican-
waves of his mind, the words blur, and are lost.

Wyoming

Who can believe in those plains
Without which the birds
Spurt right and left,
Themselves stupefied. Where

Across the spirit level
Nothing goes,
You say, nothing moving across nothing.
Try catching that now.

Try thinking calmly and solely
Of the leafless tree, without
Its splinters, without the cracks
It lends the sky

Like ceiling-plaster,
Without the great girdle
Of birds above,
Its flexing, narrowing loop?

In Absentia

Wind fails to scalp the snowfield.
Twinned cavities in winter's tusk,

we tow a spliff's gegenschein
through the trees like a trousseau.

Sometimes we find ourselves
at the edges of things –

think it possible to live
within their borders,

as sun jellies in the palette
of a puddle, or water is controlled

by the curve of a vase.
Even now, we flicker in uneven light.

It will not break.
Over the trees, until evening, starlings

wrap and unwrap themselves
in the gurning of the lockjawed lake.

A Later Stage of Discipline

Tonight, under the threshed light
of this concave city, I will underwrite
your hand-scribed manual of confidence tricks,
imported unnamed tins
of warpaint 'sunset blue', or whatever
Ponzi scheme the papilla

of your charisma might issue. Being providential,
your pince-nez was preserved
against the cataracts and hurricanoes ramming
against what, I'm afraid, has been downgraded to a wigwam;
but that's probably just today talking. Tomorrow,
or the next day, or whenever we're free,

we might gift you
an oasis diadem in gratitude
for your lifetime, and pen thirteen juicy
zebu in a tomb of gingko trees
to enshrine the legacy, known by all
to be worth the love of sustained labour. It will be official,

then unofficial. And vice versa, of course,
or even something worse. This garden, say, that currently bears
the name of some pale vessel of Paul
has a rosy fragrance, and benefits from transparent walls.
The brochure says at dusk vast
clouds of green butterfly scuttelate

the green air; plus it's patrolled
24/7 by liquorice-smoking heavies dressed
in ill-fitting zoot suits. If you can't mask your concern
that your quarters will be ransacked
while you doze, we advise you speak to the resident pescatarian,
who come rain or shine

will yammer with anyone with a smattering of Greek or Russian
about anything parched under the sun.
He's pleasant enough as long as you don't, under any circumstances,
ask if something might not change, or, worse,
require something to stay the same. If your shellacked
throat makes breathing laboured,

orderlies in pressed uniforms will be there
at the press of this white button. They
are trained not to look you straight in the eye.
They will check with a spirit level
if the bed's as flat as you say.
I can guarantee that something happens almost every day.

Remember, things will never be as bad you say.
Regardless of public holidays,
funerals of loved ones, or the arrival of the circus,
I want you to be assured
of the fact that, under no circumstance,
will any of you ever be left alone.

With Hindsight

The way to the stomach is through the heart.
If he's been eating with his eyes, ask him exactly how much
He's been beholding. If his words are drowned out
By his actions, tell him not to protest so much.

A little yearning is a dangerous thing; he clearly hasn't been
Eating his apple-a-day. If only the incision were skin-deep.
No wonder he's blind. But even a worm will turn –
Softly, softly – from a piece of string to a length of old rope.

Give him enough and he'll hang.
If God had meant us to fall, he'd have given us wings –
But then there'd be no work for drinkers.
So, those who cannot preach, practise.
Truth is wasted on the tongue.

Three Summaries

During My Time Here

I have learned that activities do not bring us closer together.
Retelling an activity creates intimacy more efficiently.
Though I understand that killing can be a powerful symbol of friendship,
the happiest marriage is only possible when the two parties do nothing together
and tell each other everything. In contrast,
a healthy father–son relationship is only possible when a) the father is
killed in the performance of an act of heroism b) the son is
killed in the performance of an act of innocence or c) they are both
alive and well, in distant parts of a country, with one or two shared
killing-fantasies to bind them together.
One of these should involve a prominent politician.
The other should involve the colour of the bathroom walls.
Neither of these should overtly address race, gender, or sexuality,
though an attitude should be permitted, if sufficiently
and, if possible, wittily, concealed. Ambiguity is the cornerstone
of a healthy dog–master relationship.

During My Time Here

I have learned to use the same muscle to care
about astronauts flying and to not care about prisoners vomiting.
Though I understand that justice can be a powerful symbol of virility,
the most satisfying sex is only possible when neither prisoner nor guard
cares if the other is satisfied. In contrast,
a healthy poet–reader relationship is only possible if a) the poet is
killed in the performance of an act of communication b) the reader is
killed in the performance of an act of understanding or c) they are both
alive and well, in distant parts of a country, with one or two shared
erotic fantasies to bind them together.
One of these should involve a prominent novelist.
The other should involve a pile of Christmas cards.
Neither of these should overtly address politics, beauty, or love,
though an attitude should be permitted, if sufficiently
and, if possible, ingeniously, feigned. Disengagement is the cornerstone
of a healthy teacher–student relationship.

During My Time Here

I have learned to speak about my desires in a way that does not embarrass
my friends, family, teachers, students, prisoners, guards and astronauts.
Though I understand that listening is a powerful symbol of desire,
the ideal audience is only possible when combining neutered pets
with archive footage. In contrast,
a healthy driver–passenger relationship is only possible if a) the driver is
killed in the performance of a swerve to avoid a child b) the passenger is
killed in the performance of oral sex upon the driver or c) they are both
alive and well, in distant parts of a country, with one or two shared
travel fantasies to bind them together.
One of these should involve adopting a child.
The other should involve several popular songs.
Neither of these should overtly address language, religion, or currency,
though an attitude should be permitted, if sufficiently
and, if possible, enthusiastically, ill-founded. Ignorance is the cornerstone
of a healthy tourist–guide relationship.

Martedì Grasso

1

An infant left unexposed
                  to linguistic stimulus
                            will automatically begin to speak
Enochian, the language
                  of the angels. Black
                            and white, boy and girl operate
in this language together.
                  One cries, 'Let this length
                            therefore be called the *Standard*; let
one Tenth of it be called
                  a *Foot*; one Tenth of a *Foot*
                            an *Inch*; one Tenth of an *Inch* a *Line*.'
Under this, gently: 'Un mecanismo
                  arbitrario de gruñidos y de
                            chillidos, so uncommon in its failure

2

angels in their tens of thousands
                  encircled the throne,
                            whispering *telocvovim*.' Soon, flames lamb
ent wrapped round Tottenham
                  and wrapped round Clapham. Before this:
                            'The restra
ints imposed by a mercantile
                  culture, ruinous
                            in effects up
on many who comprised the crowd,
                  encouraged rapid volatility.'
                            (A doctor co
unted very able / designes
                  that all Mankynd converse
                            shall.) Everything m

anifesting its own version of fullness:
          'Infra thin
                    separation betwe
en / the detonation noise of a gun / (very
          close) and the apparition
                    of the bullet / hole
in the target.' There should be a
          word that can only
                    be spoken if
one does not know what it means.
                    And these signs shall follow
                    them that believe:
(under breath) they shall cast out devils
          in my name; they shall speak
                    with new tongues…

Manna

Nothing is the same for anyone:
oil for the elderly, bread for the young, as thick as honey

on the tongue
for the thing you cannot imagine being.

When you put it in your mouth
it fits itself

to every speaker's taste:
as though the question *what is*

it is as good, as unpronounceable,
as what it is.

Old-Fashioned Uncouth Measurer

Il y a une horloge qui ne sonne pas
Arthur Rimbaud

Something clear melts where I come by – as though
I were a thing caught in the day's throat.
Through the emptier stretches rosy fluids grow dark and wet
the incessant waking, switching on light
and pointless light: jog thou on, we repeated, under
breath, towards an authentic contraption levered
high in the entrance hall –
make a habit of the stake we've all made. Still,
with hunger like a mirror persuading
we caught on to our own moving
and sought out a moisture to restore it. The span between silences
buckled in our averted nerves.
Now the breeze lifts the networks of leaves from the staircase
like your daughter's resemblances of fish.
They are, apparently, more true,
you tell me:
as in the vault of those fingers
my own was kept cold, less false.

Sphinx

Installed from sleep, I could barely register
the smallest mitigations; cries seemed sodden
in the thickening air, unable to expend themselves;
blood scalped my cheeks; each body
made a knot in the straining net. Amongst
the edges I turned and turned looking for the one
with the monastic face, whose limpid features seemed like limbs
pressing through a velvet curtain;
it was vital to know how lost, how far fallen, I shouted,
sensing a yarn unrolling ahead of me
towards the yawn of a needle-eye. Delirious,
I emptied a vial of old pollen into the wind;
one eager ephebe swiftly cut the callouses from my
fretting hand, and soundlessly dropped them in. In the crush
of eyebeams there began a slippage, gradual,
that gave off its own kind of light; as though
it were possible to look through the glowing pink of your ears
and envisage only sun after sun after sun.

Leaving the City of Acupuncture

Round days undid themselves against us.
Such windows blurred in the precision of their pixels:
How to signify what meant to you? The rain in the windows
Shaving itself new? A face remaking itself
In its own desultory image
Meant more to its landscape than you.

Through the wall of still–
Night air we read Trakl to each other, then spat on our hands,
Then leaned over the edge of the marina. The moments
Did not absorb us. We could say it again and again,
We told each other, without the meaning ever having to change
Into something that, once, might have meant the same.

Kayak

It was already late: clambering out
of the undergrowth, thirsty, sweating, lagging behind
my own thoughts, I hirpled down towards
the curve of the shore, jangling
and trailing trinkets. Above the lake,
the sky had thickened to the colour of a mirror
calloused with hothoused breath,
and everything suddenly
moved too slowly: birds swayed
their massive wings like emperors' fans; the sound
of each footfall endured a dozen
heartbeats; small waves curled across the surface of the lake
like a knife leisurely through butter. A tiny kayak
unzipped its path across it.
As I stumbled over rocks and flowers I began
to count out my steps with bites on the inside of my cheek, until,
the panicked moment the taste of blood
hit my tongue, I found myself wanting to call out
through the loudspeaker of my funnelled hands
the name of the figure rocking in the kayak, who was leaning
his lucent body over, now, as if to fish something floating
out of the clearing water,
as if to see what he could see
beyond the valve of his own reflection.

Notes

p. 12   'The Inability to Recall the Precise Word for Something' is a found poem, found here: http://users.tinyonline.co.uk/gswithenbank/unuwords.htm

p. 53   'Martedi Grasso' combines elements of the writing of Jorge Luis Borges, Marcel Duchamp and Peter Ackroyd, among others, with excerpts from David Starkey's contribution to *Newsnight* in July 2011.